BE SOBER

This Journal Belongs To

_____

_____

_____

Date: _____

Mon ☐ Tues ☐ Wednes ☐ Thurs ☐ Fri ☐ Satur ☐ Sun ☐

One Goal For Today: _____

_____

_____

Today's Postive Affirmations: _____

_____

_____

_____

_____

My Mood Today: ⭐ ⭐ ⭐ ⭐ ⭐ ⭐ ⭐ ⭐ ⭐ ⭐

My Thoughts For Today: _____

_____

_____

_____

_____

What Am I Grateful For Today: _____

_____

_____

_____

What I Am Proud Of Today: _____

_____

_____

_____

My Plans For Tomorrow: _____

_____

_____

_____

Date: _____

Mon ☐ Tues ☐ Wednes ☐ Thurs ☐ Fri ☐ Satur ☐ Sun ☐

One Goal For Today: _____

_____

_____

Today's Postive Affirmations: _____

_____

_____

_____

My Mood Today: ⭐ ⭐ ⭐ ⭐ ⭐ ⭐ ⭐ ⭐ ⭐

My Thoughts For Today: _____

_____

_____

_____

_____

What Am I Grateful For Today: _____

_____

_____

_____

What I Am Proud Of Today: _____

_____

_____

_____

My Plans For Tomorrow: _____

_____

_____

_____

Date: _____

Mon ☐ Tues ☐ Wednes ☐ Thurs ☐ Fri ☐ Satur ☐ Sun ☐

One Goal For Today: _____

_____

_____

Today's Postive Affirmations: _____

_____

_____

_____

_____

My Mood Today: ★ ★ ★ ★ ★ ★ ★ ★ ★ ★

My Thoughts For Today: _____

_____

_____

_____

_____

What Am I Grateful For Today: _____

_____

_____

_____

What I Am Proud Of Today: _____

_____

_____

_____

My Plans For Tomorrow: _____

_____

_____

_____

Date: _____

Mon ☐ Tues ☐ Wednes ☐ Thurs ☐ Fri ☐ Satur ☐ Sun ☐

One Goal For Today: _____

_____

_____

Today's Postive Affirmations: _____

_____

_____

_____

_____

My Mood Today: ☆ ☆ ☆ ☆ ☆ ☆ ☆ ☆ ☆ ☆

My Thoughts For Today: _____

_____

_____

_____

_____

What Am I Grateful For Today: _____

_____

_____

_____

What I Am Proud Of Today: _____

_____

_____

_____

My Plans For Tomorrow: _____

_____

_____

_____

Date: _____

Mon ☐ Tues ☐ Wednes ☐ Thurs ☐ Fri ☐ Satur ☐ Sun ☐

One Goal For Today: _____

_____

_____

Today's Postive Affirmations: _____

_____

_____

_____

_____

My Mood Today: ★ ★ ★ ★ ★ ★ ★ ★ ★ ★

My Thoughts For Today: _____

_____

_____

_____

_____

What Am I Grateful For Today: _____

_____

_____

_____

What I Am Proud Of Today: _____

_____

_____

_____

My Plans For Tomorrow: _____

_____

_____

_____

Date: _____

Mon ☐ Tues ☐ Wednes ☐ Thurs ☐ Fri ☐ Satur ☐ Sun ☐

One Goal For Today: _____

_____

_____

Today's Postive Affirmations: _____

_____

_____

_____

_____

My Mood Today: ☆ ☆ ☆ ☆ ☆ ☆ ☆ ☆ ☆ ☆

My Thoughts For Today: _____

_____

_____

_____

_____

What Am I Grateful For Today: _____

_____

_____

_____

What I Am Proud Of Today: _____

_____

_____

_____

My Plans For Tomorrow: _____

_____

_____

_____

Date: _____

Mon ☐ Tues ☐ Wednes ☐ Thurs ☐ Fri ☐ Satur ☐ Sun ☐

One Goal For Today: _____

_____

_____

Today's Postive Affirmations: _____

_____

_____

_____

My Mood Today: ★ ★ ★ ★ ★ ★ ★ ★ ★ ★

My Thoughts For Today: _____

_____

_____

_____

_____

What Am I Grateful For Today: _____

_____

_____

_____

What I Am Proud Of Today: _____

_____

_____

_____

My Plans For Tomorrow: _____

_____

_____

_____

Date: _____

Mon ☐ Tues ☐ Wednes ☐ Thurs ☐ Fri ☐ Satur ☐ Sun ☐

One Goal For Today: _____

_____

_____

Today's Postive Affirmations: _____

_____

_____

_____

_____

My Mood Today: ☆ ☆ ☆ ☆ ☆ ☆ ☆ ☆ ☆ ☆

My Thoughts For Today: _____

_____

_____

_____

_____

What Am I Grateful For Today: _____

_____

_____

_____

What I Am Proud Of Today: _____

_____

_____

_____

My Plans For Tomorrow: _____

_____

_____

_____

Date: _____

Mon ☐ Tues ☐ Wednes ☐ Thurs ☐ Fri ☐ Satur ☐ Sun ☐

One Goal For Today: _____

_____

_____

Today's Postive Affirmations: _____

_____

_____

_____

_____

My Mood Today: ☆ ☆ ☆ ☆ ☆ ☆ ☆ ☆ ☆ ☆

My Thoughts For Today: _____

_____

_____

_____

_____

What Am I Grateful For Today: _____

_____

_____

_____

What I Am Proud Of Today: _____

_____

_____

_____

My Plans For Tomorrow: _____

_____

_____

_____

Date: _____

Mon ☐ Tues ☐ Wednes ☐ Thurs ☐ Fri ☐ Satur ☐ Sun ☐

One Goal For Today: _____

_____

_____

Today's Postive Affirmations: _____

_____

_____

_____

_____

My Mood Today: ☆ ☆ ☆ ☆ ☆ ☆ ☆ ☆ ☆ ☆

My Thoughts For Today: _____

_____

_____

_____

_____

What Am I Grateful For Today: _____

_____

_____

_____

What I Am Proud Of Today: _____

_____

_____

_____

My Plans For Tomorrow: _____

_____

_____

_____

Date: _____

Mon ☐ Tues ☐ Wednes ☐ Thurs ☐ Fri ☐ Satur ☐ Sun ☐

One Goal For Today: _____

_____

_____

Today's Postive Affirmations: _____

_____

_____

_____

_____

My Mood Today: ☆ ☆ ☆ ☆ ☆ ☆ ☆ ☆ ☆ ☆

My Thoughts For Today: _____

_____

_____

_____

_____

What Am I Grateful For Today: _____

_____

_____

_____

What I Am Proud Of Today: _____

_____

_____

_____

My Plans For Tomorrow: _____

_____

_____

_____

Date: _____

Mon ☐ Tues ☐ Wednes ☐ Thurs ☐ Fri ☐ Satur ☐ Sun ☐

One Goal For Today: _____

_____

_____

Today's Postive Affirmations: _____

_____

_____

_____

_____

My Mood Today: ⭐ ⭐ ⭐ ⭐ ⭐ ⭐ ⭐ ⭐ ⭐

My Thoughts For Today: _____

_____

_____

_____

_____

What Am I Grateful For Today: _____

_____

_____

_____

What I Am Proud Of Today: _____

_____

_____

_____

My Plans For Tomorrow: _____

_____

_____

_____

Date: _____

Mon ☐ Tues ☐ Wednes ☐ Thurs ☐ Fri ☐ Satur ☐ Sun ☐

One Goal For Today: _____

_____

_____

Today's Postive Affirmations: _____

_____

_____

_____

_____

My Mood Today: ⭐ ⭐ ⭐ ⭐ ⭐ ⭐ ⭐ ⭐ ⭐

My Thoughts For Today: _____

_____

_____

_____

_____

What Am I Grateful For Today: _____

_____

_____

_____

What I Am Proud Of Today: _____

_____

_____

_____

My Plans For Tomorrow: _____

_____

_____

_____

Date: _____

Mon ☐ Tues ☐ Wednes ☐ Thurs ☐ Fri ☐ Satur ☐ Sun ☐

One Goal For Today: _____

_____

_____

Today's Postive Affirmations: _____

_____

_____

_____

_____

My Mood Today: ☆ ☆ ☆ ☆ ☆ ☆ ☆ ☆ ☆

My Thoughts For Today: _____

_____

_____

_____

_____

What Am I Grateful For Today: _____

_____

_____

_____

What I Am Proud Of Today: _____

_____

_____

_____

My Plans For Tomorrow: _____

_____

_____

_____

Date: _____

Mon ☐ Tues ☐ Wednes ☐ Thurs ☐ Fri ☐ Satur ☐ Sun ☐

One Goal For Today: _____

_____

_____

Today's Postive Affirmations: _____

_____

_____

_____

_____

My Mood Today: ⭐ ⭐ ⭐ ⭐ ⭐ ⭐ ⭐ ⭐ ⭐ ⭐

My Thoughts For Today: _____

_____

_____

_____

_____

What Am I Grateful For Today: _____

_____

_____

_____

What I Am Proud Of Today: _____

_____

_____

_____

My Plans For Tomorrow: _____

_____

_____

_____

Date: _____

Mon ☐ Tues ☐ Wednes ☐ Thurs ☐ Fri ☐ Satur ☐ Sun ☐

One Goal For Today: _____

_____

_____

Today's Postive Affirmations: _____

_____

_____

_____

_____

My Mood Today: ★ ★ ★ ★ ★ ★ ★ ★ ★ ★

My Thoughts For Today: _____

_____

_____

_____

_____

What Am I Grateful For Today: _____

_____

_____

_____

What I Am Proud Of Today: _____

_____

_____

_____

My Plans For Tomorrow: _____

_____

_____

_____

Date: _____

Mon ☐ Tues ☐ Wednes ☐ Thurs ☐ Fri ☐ Satur ☐ Sun ☐

One Goal For Today: _____
_____
_____

Today's Postive Affirmations: _____
_____
_____
_____
_____

My Mood Today: ☆ ☆ ☆ ☆ ☆ ☆ ☆ ☆ ☆

My Thoughts For Today: _____
_____
_____
_____
_____

What Am I Grateful For Today: _____
_____
_____
_____

What I Am Proud Of Today: _____
_____
_____
_____

My Plans For Tomorrow: _____
_____
_____
_____

Date: _____

Mon ☐ Tues ☐ Wednes ☐ Thurs ☐ Fri ☐ Satur ☐ Sun ☐

One Goal For Today: _____

_____

_____

Today's Postive Affirmations: _____

_____

_____

_____

_____

My Mood Today: ☆ ☆ ☆ ☆ ☆ ☆ ☆ ☆ ☆ ☆

My Thoughts For Today: _____

_____

_____

_____

_____

What Am I Grateful For Today: _____

_____

_____

_____

What I Am Proud Of Today: _____

_____

_____

_____

My Plans For Tomorrow: _____

_____

_____

_____

Date: _____

Mon ☐ Tues ☐ Wednes ☐ Thurs ☐ Fri ☐ Satur ☐ Sun ☐

One Goal For Today: _____

_____

_____

Today's Postive Affirmations: _____

_____

_____

_____

_____

My Mood Today: ⭐ ⭐ ⭐ ⭐ ⭐ ⭐ ⭐ ⭐ ⭐ ⭐

My Thoughts For Today: _____

_____

_____

_____

_____

What Am I Grateful For Today: _____

_____

_____

_____

What I Am Proud Of Today: _____

_____

_____

_____

My Plans For Tomorrow: _____

_____

_____

_____

Date: _____

Mon ☐ Tues ☐ Wednes ☐ Thurs ☐ Fri ☐ Satur ☐ Sun ☐

One Goal For Today: _____

_____

_____

Today's Postive Affirmations: _____

_____

_____

_____

_____

My Mood Today: ⭐ ⭐ ⭐ ⭐ ⭐ ⭐ ⭐ ⭐ ⭐ ⭐

My Thoughts For Today: _____

_____

_____

_____

_____

What Am I Grateful For Today: _____

_____

_____

_____

What I Am Proud Of Today: _____

_____

_____

_____

My Plans For Tomorrow: _____

_____

_____

_____

Date: _____

Mon ☐ Tues ☐ Wednes ☐ Thurs ☐ Fri ☐ Satur ☐ Sun ☐

One Goal For Today: _____

_____

_____

Today's Postive Affirmations: _____

_____

_____

_____

_____

My Mood Today: ⭐ ⭐ ⭐ ⭐ ⭐ ⭐ ⭐ ⭐ ⭐ ⭐

My Thoughts For Today: _____

_____

_____

_____

_____

What Am I Grateful For Today: _____

_____

_____

_____

What I Am Proud Of Today: _____

_____

_____

_____

My Plans For Tomorrow: _____

_____

_____

_____

Date: _____

Mon ☐ Tues ☐ Wednes ☐ Thurs ☐ Fri ☐ Satur ☐ Sun ☐

One Goal For Today: _____
_____
_____

Today's Postive Affirmations: _____
_____
_____
_____
_____

My Mood Today: ☆ ☆ ☆ ☆ ☆ ☆ ☆ ☆ ☆

My Thoughts For Today: _____
_____
_____
_____
_____

What Am I Grateful For Today: _____
_____
_____
_____

What I Am Proud Of Today: _____
_____
_____
_____

My Plans For Tomorrow: _____
_____
_____
_____

Date: _____

Mon ☐ Tues ☐ Wednes ☐ Thurs ☐ Fri ☐ Satur ☐ Sun ☐

One Goal For Today: _____

_____

_____

Today's Postive Affirmations: _____

_____

_____

_____

_____

My Mood Today: ☆ ☆ ☆ ☆ ☆ ☆ ☆ ☆ ☆ ☆

My Thoughts For Today: _____

_____

_____

_____

_____

What Am I Grateful For Today: _____

_____

_____

_____

What I Am Proud Of Today: _____

_____

_____

_____

My Plans For Tomorrow: _____

_____

_____

_____

Date: _____
Mon ☐ Tues ☐ Wednes ☐ Thurs ☐ Fri ☐ Satur ☐ Sun ☐

One Goal For Today: _____
_____
_____

Today's Postive Affirmations: _____
_____
_____
_____
_____

My Mood Today: ☆ ☆ ☆ ☆ ☆ ☆ ☆ ☆ ☆ ☆

My Thoughts For Today: _____
_____
_____
_____
_____

What Am I Grateful For Today: _____
_____
_____
_____

What I Am Proud Of Today: _____
_____
_____
_____

My Plans For Tomorrow: _____
_____
_____
_____

Date: _____

Mon ☐ Tues ☐ Wednes ☐ Thurs ☐ Fri ☐ Satur ☐ Sun ☐

One Goal For Today: _____
_____
_____

Today's Postive Affirmations: _____
_____
_____
_____
_____

My Mood Today: ⭐ ⭐ ⭐ ⭐ ⭐ ⭐ ⭐ ⭐ ⭐ ⭐

My Thoughts For Today: _____
_____
_____
_____
_____

What Am I Grateful For Today: _____
_____
_____
_____

What I Am Proud Of Today: _____
_____
_____
_____

My Plans For Tomorrow: _____
_____
_____
_____

Date: _____

Mon ☐ Tues ☐ Wednes ☐ Thurs ☐ Fri ☐ Satur ☐ Sun ☐

One Goal For Today: _____

_____

_____

Today's Postive Affirmations: _____

_____

_____

_____

My Mood Today: ☆ ☆ ☆ ☆ ☆ ☆ ☆ ☆

My Thoughts For Today: _____

_____

_____

_____

_____

What Am I Grateful For Today: _____

_____

_____

_____

What I Am Proud Of Today: _____

_____

_____

_____

My Plans For Tomorrow: _____

_____

_____

_____

Date: _____

Mon ☐ Tues ☐ Wednes ☐ Thurs ☐ Fri ☐ Satur ☐ Sun ☐

One Goal For Today: _____

_____

_____

Today's Postive Affirmations: _____

_____

_____

_____

_____

My Mood Today: ☆ ☆ ☆ ☆ ☆ ☆ ☆ ☆ ☆ ☆

My Thoughts For Today: _____

_____

_____

_____

_____

What Am I Grateful For Today: _____

_____

_____

_____

What I Am Proud Of Today: _____

_____

_____

_____

My Plans For Tomorrow: _____

_____

_____

_____

Date: _____

Mon ☐ Tues ☐ Wednes ☐ Thurs ☐ Fri ☐ Satur ☐ Sun ☐

One Goal For Today: _____

_____

_____

Today's Postive Affirmations: _____

_____

_____

_____

_____

My Mood Today: ★ ★ ★ ★ ★ ★ ★ ★ ★

My Thoughts For Today: _____

_____

_____

_____

_____

What Am I Grateful For Today: _____

_____

_____

_____

What I Am Proud Of Today: _____

_____

_____

_____

My Plans For Tomorrow: _____

_____

_____

_____

Date: _____

Mon ☐ Tues ☐ Wednes ☐ Thurs ☐ Fri ☐ Satur ☐ Sun ☐

One Goal For Today: _____

_____

_____

Today's Postive Affirmations: _____

_____

_____

_____

_____

My Mood Today: ☆ ☆ ☆ ☆ ☆ ☆ ☆ ☆ ☆ ☆

My Thoughts For Today: _____

_____

_____

_____

_____

What Am I Grateful For Today: _____

_____

_____

_____

What I Am Proud Of Today: _____

_____

_____

_____

My Plans For Tomorrow: _____

_____

_____

_____

Date: _____

Mon ☐ Tues ☐ Wednes ☐ Thurs ☐ Fri ☐ Satur ☐ Sun ☐

One Goal For Today: _____

_____

_____

Today's Postive Affirmations: _____

_____

_____

_____

_____

My Mood Today: ★ ★ ★ ★ ★ ★ ★ ★ ★ ★

My Thoughts For Today: _____

_____

_____

_____

_____

What Am I Grateful For Today: _____

_____

_____

_____

What I Am Proud Of Today: _____

_____

_____

_____

My Plans For Tomorrow: _____

_____

_____

_____

Date: _____

Mon ☐ Tues ☐ Wednes ☐ Thurs ☐ Fri ☐ Satur ☐ Sun ☐

One Goal For Today: _____
_____
_____

Today's Postive Affirmations: _____
_____
_____
_____
_____

My Mood Today: ☆ ☆ ☆ ☆ ☆ ☆ ☆ ☆ ☆ ☆

My Thoughts For Today: _____
_____
_____
_____
_____

What Am I Grateful For Today: _____
_____
_____
_____

What I Am Proud Of Today: _____
_____
_____
_____

My Plans For Tomorrow: _____
_____
_____
_____

Date: _____

Mon ☐ Tues ☐ Wednes ☐ Thurs ☐ Fri ☐ Satur ☐ Sun ☐

One Goal For Today: _____
_____
_____

Today's Postive Affirmations: _____
_____
_____
_____
_____

My Mood Today: ☆ ☆ ☆ ☆ ☆ ☆ ☆ ☆ ☆ ☆

My Thoughts For Today: _____
_____
_____
_____
_____

What Am I Grateful For Today: _____
_____
_____
_____

What I Am Proud Of Today: _____
_____
_____
_____

My Plans For Tomorrow: _____
_____
_____
_____

Date: _____

Mon ☐ Tues ☐ Wednes ☐ Thurs ☐ Fri ☐ Satur ☐ Sun ☐

One Goal For Today: _____
_____
_____

Today's Postive Affirmations: _____
_____
_____
_____
_____

My Mood Today: ★ ★ ★ ★ ★ ★ ★ ★ ★ ★

My Thoughts For Today: _____
_____
_____
_____
_____

What Am I Grateful For Today: _____
_____
_____
_____

What I Am Proud Of Today: _____
_____
_____
_____

My Plans For Tomorrow: _____
_____
_____
_____

Date: _____

Mon ☐ Tues ☐ Wednes ☐ Thurs ☐ Fri ☐ Satur ☐ Sun ☐

One Goal For Today: _____

_____

_____

Today's Postive Affirmations: _____

_____

_____

_____

_____

My Mood Today: ☆ ☆ ☆ ☆ ☆ ☆ ☆ ☆ ☆ ☆

My Thoughts For Today: _____

_____

_____

_____

_____

What Am I Grateful For Today: _____

_____

_____

_____

What I Am Proud Of Today: _____

_____

_____

_____

My Plans For Tomorrow: _____

_____

_____

_____

Date: _____

Mon ☐ Tues ☐ Wednes ☐ Thurs ☐ Fri ☐ Satur ☐ Sun ☐

One Goal For Today: _____

_____

_____

Today's Postive Affirmations: _____

_____

_____

_____

_____

My Mood Today: ★ ★ ★ ★ ★ ★ ★ ★ ★ ★

My Thoughts For Today: _____

_____

_____

_____

_____

What Am I Grateful For Today: _____

_____

_____

_____

What I Am Proud Of Today: _____

_____

_____

_____

My Plans For Tomorrow: _____

_____

_____

_____

Date: _____

Mon ☐ Tues ☐ Wednes ☐ Thurs ☐ Fri ☐ Satur ☐ Sun ☐

One Goal For Today: _____
_____
_____

Today's Postive Affirmations: _____
_____
_____
_____
_____

My Mood Today: ☆ ☆ ☆ ☆ ☆ ☆ ☆ ☆ ☆ ☆

My Thoughts For Today: _____
_____
_____
_____
_____

What Am I Grateful For Today: _____
_____
_____
_____

What I Am Proud Of Today: _____
_____
_____
_____

My Plans For Tomorrow: _____
_____
_____
_____

Date: _____

Mon ☐ Tues ☐ Wednes ☐ Thurs ☐ Fri ☐ Satur ☐ Sun ☐

One Goal For Today: _____

_____

_____

Today's Postive Affirmations: _____

_____

_____

_____

_____

My Mood Today: ☆ ☆ ☆ ☆ ☆ ☆ ☆ ☆ ☆ ☆

My Thoughts For Today: _____

_____

_____

_____

_____

What Am I Grateful For Today: _____

_____

_____

_____

What I Am Proud Of Today: _____

_____

_____

_____

My Plans For Tomorrow: _____

_____

_____

_____

Date: _____

Mon ☐ Tues ☐ Wednes ☐ Thurs ☐ Fri ☐ Satur ☐ Sun ☐

One Goal For Today: _____

_____

_____

Today's Postive Affirmations: _____

_____

_____

_____

_____

My Mood Today: ⭐ ⭐ ⭐ ⭐ ⭐ ⭐ ⭐ ⭐

My Thoughts For Today: _____

_____

_____

_____

_____

What Am I Grateful For Today: _____

_____

_____

_____

What I Am Proud Of Today: _____

_____

_____

_____

My Plans For Tomorrow: _____

_____

_____

_____

Date: _____

Mon ☐ Tues ☐ Wednes ☐ Thurs ☐ Fri ☐ Satur ☐ Sun ☐

One Goal For Today: _____

_____

_____

Today's Postive Affirmations: _____

_____

_____

_____

_____

My Mood Today: ★ ★ ★ ★ ★ ★ ★ ★ ★ ★

My Thoughts For Today: _____

_____

_____

_____

_____

What Am I Grateful For Today: _____

_____

_____

_____

What I Am Proud Of Today: _____

_____

_____

_____

My Plans For Tomorrow: _____

_____

_____

_____

Date: _____

Mon ☐ Tues ☐ Wednes ☐ Thurs ☐ Fri ☐ Satur ☐ Sun ☐

One Goal For Today: _____

_____

_____

Today's Postive Affirmations: _____

_____

_____

_____

_____

My Mood Today: ☆ ☆ ☆ ☆ ☆ ☆ ☆ ☆ ☆

My Thoughts For Today: _____

_____

_____

_____

_____

What Am I Grateful For Today: _____

_____

_____

_____

What I Am Proud Of Today: _____

_____

_____

_____

My Plans For Tomorrow: _____

_____

_____

_____

Date: _____

Mon ☐ Tues ☐ Wednes ☐ Thurs ☐ Fri ☐ Satur ☐ Sun ☐

One Goal For Today: _____

_____

_____

Today's Postive Affirmations: _____

_____

_____

_____

_____

My Mood Today: ★ ★ ★ ★ ★ ★ ★ ★ ★ ★

My Thoughts For Today: _____

_____

_____

_____

_____

What Am I Grateful For Today: _____

_____

_____

_____

What I Am Proud Of Today: _____

_____

_____

_____

My Plans For Tomorrow: _____

_____

_____

_____

Date: _____

Mon ☐ Tues ☐ Wednes ☐ Thurs ☐ Fri ☐ Satur ☐ Sun ☐

One Goal For Today: _____

_____

_____

Today's Postive Affirmations: _____

_____

_____

_____

_____

My Mood Today: ☆ ☆ ☆ ☆ ☆ ☆ ☆ ☆ ☆

My Thoughts For Today: _____

_____

_____

_____

_____

What Am I Grateful For Today: _____

_____

_____

_____

What I Am Proud Of Today: _____

_____

_____

_____

My Plans For Tomorrow: _____

_____

_____

_____

Date: _____

Mon ☐ Tues ☐ Wednes ☐ Thurs ☐ Fri ☐ Satur ☐ Sun ☐

One Goal For Today: _____

_____

_____

Today's Postive Affirmations: _____

_____

_____

_____

_____

My Mood Today: ★ ★ ★ ★ ★ ★ ★ ★ ★ ★

My Thoughts For Today: _____

_____

_____

_____

_____

What Am I Grateful For Today: _____

_____

_____

_____

What I Am Proud Of Today: _____

_____

_____

_____

My Plans For Tomorrow: _____

_____

_____

_____

Date: _____

Mon ☐ Tues ☐ Wednes ☐ Thurs ☐ Fri ☐ Satur ☐ Sun ☐

One Goal For Today: _____
_____
_____

Today's Postive Affirmations: _____
_____
_____
_____
_____

My Mood Today: ☆ ☆ ☆ ☆ ☆ ☆ ☆ ☆ ☆ ☆

My Thoughts For Today: _____
_____
_____
_____
_____

What Am I Grateful For Today: _____
_____
_____
_____

What I Am Proud Of Today: _____
_____
_____
_____

My Plans For Tomorrow: _____
_____
_____
_____

Date: _____

Mon ☐ Tues ☐ Wednes ☐ Thurs ☐ Fri ☐ Satur ☐ Sun ☐

One Goal For Today: _____

_____

_____

Today's Postive Affirmations: _____

_____

_____

_____

_____

My Mood Today: ⭐ ⭐ ⭐ ⭐ ⭐ ⭐ ⭐ ⭐ ⭐ ⭐

My Thoughts For Today: _____

_____

_____

_____

_____

What Am I Grateful For Today: _____

_____

_____

_____

What I Am Proud Of Today: _____

_____

_____

_____

My Plans For Tomorrow: _____

_____

_____

_____

Date: _____

Mon ☐　Tues ☐　Wednes ☐　Thurs ☐　Fri ☐　Satur ☐　Sun ☐

One Goal For Today: _____

_____

_____

Today's Postive Affirmations: _____

_____

_____

_____

_____

My Mood Today:　☆　☆　☆　☆　☆　☆　☆　☆　☆

My Thoughts For Today: _____

_____

_____

_____

_____

What Am I Grateful For Today: _____

_____

_____

_____

What I Am Proud Of Today: _____

_____

_____

_____

My Plans For Tomorrow: _____

_____

_____

_____

Date: _____

Mon ☐ Tues ☐ Wednes ☐ Thurs ☐ Fri ☐ Satur ☐ Sun ☐

One Goal For Today: _____

_____

_____

Today's Postive Affirmations: _____

_____

_____

_____

My Mood Today: ☆ ☆ ☆ ☆ ☆ ☆ ☆ ☆ ☆ ☆

My Thoughts For Today: _____

_____

_____

_____

_____

What Am I Grateful For Today: _____

_____

_____

_____

What I Am Proud Of Today: _____

_____

_____

_____

My Plans For Tomorrow: _____

_____

_____

_____

Date: _____

Mon ☐ Tues ☐ Wednes ☐ Thurs ☐ Fri ☐ Satur ☐ Sun ☐

One Goal For Today: _____

_____

_____

Today's Postive Affirmations: _____

_____

_____

_____

_____

My Mood Today: ☆ ☆ ☆ ☆ ☆ ☆ ☆ ☆ ☆

My Thoughts For Today: _____

_____

_____

_____

_____

What Am I Grateful For Today: _____

_____

_____

_____

What I Am Proud Of Today: _____

_____

_____

_____

My Plans For Tomorrow: _____

_____

_____

_____

Date: _____

Mon ☐ Tues ☐ Wednes ☐ Thurs ☐ Fri ☐ Satur ☐ Sun ☐

One Goal For Today: _____

_____

_____

Today's Postive Affirmations: _____

_____

_____

_____

_____

My Mood Today: ☆ ☆ ☆ ☆ ☆ ☆ ☆ ☆ ☆ ☆

My Thoughts For Today: _____

_____

_____

_____

_____

What Am I Grateful For Today: _____

_____

_____

_____

What I Am Proud Of Today: _____

_____

_____

_____

My Plans For Tomorrow: _____

_____

_____

_____

Date: _____

Mon ☐ Tues ☐ Wednes ☐ Thurs ☐ Fri ☐ Satur ☐ Sun ☐

One Goal For Today: _____

_____

_____

Today's Postive Affirmations: _____

_____

_____

_____

My Mood Today: ★ ★ ★ ★ ★ ★ ★ ★ ★ ★

My Thoughts For Today: _____

_____

_____

_____

_____

What Am I Grateful For Today: _____

_____

_____

_____

What I Am Proud Of Today: _____

_____

_____

_____

My Plans For Tomorrow: _____

_____

_____

_____

Date: _____

Mon ☐ Tues ☐ Wednes ☐ Thurs ☐ Fri ☐ Satur ☐ Sun ☐

One Goal For Today: _____

_____

_____

Today's Postive Affirmations: _____

_____

_____

_____

_____

My Mood Today: ★ ★ ★ ★ ★ ★ ★ ★ ★ ★

My Thoughts For Today: _____

_____

_____

_____

_____

What Am I Grateful For Today: _____

_____

_____

_____

What I Am Proud Of Today: _____

_____

_____

_____

My Plans For Tomorrow: _____

_____

_____

_____

Date: _____

Mon ☐ Tues ☐ Wednes ☐ Thurs ☐ Fri ☐ Satur ☐ Sun ☐

One Goal For Today: _____

_____

_____

Today's Postive Affirmations: _____

_____

_____

_____

_____

My Mood Today: ★ ★ ★ ★ ★ ★ ★ ★ ★

My Thoughts For Today: _____

_____

_____

_____

_____

What Am I Grateful For Today: _____

_____

_____

_____

What I Am Proud Of Today: _____

_____

_____

_____

My Plans For Tomorrow: _____

_____

_____

_____

Date: _____

Mon ☐ Tues ☐ Wednes ☐ Thurs ☐ Fri ☐ Satur ☐ Sun ☐

One Goal For Today: _____
_____
_____

Today's Postive Affirmations: _____
_____
_____
_____
_____

My Mood Today: ★ ★ ★ ★ ★ ★ ★ ★ ★ ★

My Thoughts For Today: _____
_____
_____
_____
_____

What Am I Grateful For Today: _____
_____
_____
_____

What I Am Proud Of Today: _____
_____
_____
_____

My Plans For Tomorrow: _____
_____
_____
_____

Date: _____

Mon ☐ Tues ☐ Wednes ☐ Thurs ☐ Fri ☐ Satur ☐ Sun ☐

One Goal For Today: _____

_____

_____

Today's Postive Affirmations: _____

_____

_____

_____

_____

My Mood Today: ⭐ ⭐ ⭐ ⭐ ⭐ ⭐ ⭐ ⭐ ⭐ ⭐

My Thoughts For Today: _____

_____

_____

_____

_____

What Am I Grateful For Today: _____

_____

_____

_____

What I Am Proud Of Today: _____

_____

_____

_____

My Plans For Tomorrow: _____

_____

_____

_____

Date: _____

Mon ☐ Tues ☐ Wednes ☐ Thurs ☐ Fri ☐ Satur ☐ Sun ☐

One Goal For Today: _____

_____

_____

Today's Postive Affirmations: _____

_____

_____

_____

_____

My Mood Today: ☆ ☆ ☆ ☆ ☆ ☆ ☆ ☆ ☆ ☆

My Thoughts For Today: _____

_____

_____

_____

_____

What Am I Grateful For Today: _____

_____

_____

_____

What I Am Proud Of Today: _____

_____

_____

_____

My Plans For Tomorrow: _____

_____

_____

_____

Date: _____

Mon ☐ Tues ☐ Wednes ☐ Thurs ☐ Fri ☐ Satur ☐ Sun ☐

One Goal For Today: _____

_____

_____

Today's Postive Affirmations: _____

_____

_____

_____

My Mood Today: ☆ ☆ ☆ ☆ ☆ ☆ ☆ ☆ ☆ ☆

My Thoughts For Today: _____

_____

_____

_____

_____

What Am I Grateful For Today: _____

_____

_____

_____

What I Am Proud Of Today: _____

_____

_____

_____

My Plans For Tomorrow: _____

_____

_____

_____

Date: _____

Mon ☐ Tues ☐ Wednes ☐ Thurs ☐ Fri ☐ Satur ☐ Sun ☐

One Goal For Today: _____

_____

_____

Today's Postive Affirmations: _____

_____

_____

_____

_____

My Mood Today: ★ ★ ★ ★ ★ ★ ★ ★ ★ ★

My Thoughts For Today: _____

_____

_____

_____

_____

What Am I Grateful For Today: _____

_____

_____

_____

What I Am Proud Of Today: _____

_____

_____

_____

My Plans For Tomorrow: _____

_____

_____

_____

Date: _____

Mon ☐ Tues ☐ Wednes ☐ Thurs ☐ Fri ☐ Satur ☐ Sun ☐

One Goal For Today: _____

_____

_____

Today's Postive Affirmations: _____

_____

_____

_____

_____

My Mood Today: ☆ ☆ ☆ ☆ ☆ ☆ ☆ ☆ ☆

My Thoughts For Today: _____

_____

_____

_____

_____

What Am I Grateful For Today: _____

_____

_____

_____

What I Am Proud Of Today: _____

_____

_____

_____

My Plans For Tomorrow: _____

_____

_____

_____

Date: _____

Mon ☐ Tues ☐ Wednes ☐ Thurs ☐ Fri ☐ Satur ☐ Sun ☐

One Goal For Today: _____

_____

_____

Today's Postive Affirmations: _____

_____

_____

_____

_____

My Mood Today: ⭐ ⭐ ⭐ ⭐ ⭐ ⭐ ⭐ ⭐ ⭐ ⭐

My Thoughts For Today: _____

_____

_____

_____

_____

What Am I Grateful For Today: _____

_____

_____

_____

What I Am Proud Of Today: _____

_____

_____

_____

My Plans For Tomorrow: _____

_____

_____

_____

Date: _____

Mon ☐ Tues ☐ Wednes ☐ Thurs ☐ Fri ☐ Satur ☐ Sun ☐

One Goal For Today: _____

_____

_____

Today's Postive Affirmations: _____

_____

_____

_____

_____

My Mood Today: ☆ ☆ ☆ ☆ ☆ ☆ ☆ ☆ ☆

My Thoughts For Today: _____

_____

_____

_____

_____

What Am I Grateful For Today: _____

_____

_____

_____

What I Am Proud Of Today: _____

_____

_____

_____

My Plans For Tomorrow: _____

_____

_____

_____

Date: _____

Mon ☐ Tues ☐ Wednes ☐ Thurs ☐ Fri ☐ Satur ☐ Sun ☐

One Goal For Today: _____

_____

_____

Today's Postive Affirmations: _____

_____

_____

_____

_____

My Mood Today: ★ ★ ★ ★ ★ ★ ★ ★ ★ ★

My Thoughts For Today: _____

_____

_____

_____

_____

What Am I Grateful For Today: _____

_____

_____

_____

What I Am Proud Of Today: _____

_____

_____

_____

My Plans For Tomorrow: _____

_____

_____

_____

Date: _____

Mon ☐ Tues ☐ Wednes ☐ Thurs ☐ Fri ☐ Satur ☐ Sun ☐

One Goal For Today: _____

_____

_____

Today's Postive Affirmations: _____

_____

_____

_____

My Mood Today: ☆ ☆ ☆ ☆ ☆ ☆ ☆ ☆ ☆ ☆

My Thoughts For Today: _____

_____

_____

_____

_____

What Am I Grateful For Today: _____

_____

_____

_____

What I Am Proud Of Today: _____

_____

_____

_____

My Plans For Tomorrow: _____

_____

_____

_____

Date: _____

Mon ☐ Tues ☐ Wednes ☐ Thurs ☐ Fri ☐ Satur ☐ Sun ☐

One Goal For Today: _____

_____

_____

Today's Postive Affirmations: _____

_____

_____

_____

_____

My Mood Today: ⭐ ⭐ ⭐ ⭐ ⭐ ⭐ ⭐ ⭐ ⭐ ⭐

My Thoughts For Today: _____

_____

_____

_____

_____

What Am I Grateful For Today: _____

_____

_____

_____

What I Am Proud Of Today: _____

_____

_____

_____

My Plans For Tomorrow: _____

_____

_____

_____

Date: _____

Mon ☐ Tues ☐ Wednes ☐ Thurs ☐ Fri ☐ Satur ☐ Sun ☐

One Goal For Today: _____

_____

_____

Today's Postive Affirmations: _____

_____

_____

_____

_____

My Mood Today: ☆ ☆ ☆ ☆ ☆ ☆ ☆ ☆ ☆ ☆

My Thoughts For Today: _____

_____

_____

_____

_____

What Am I Grateful For Today: _____

_____

_____

_____

What I Am Proud Of Today: _____

_____

_____

_____

My Plans For Tomorrow: _____

_____

_____

_____

Date: _____

Mon ☐ Tues ☐ Wednes ☐ Thurs ☐ Fri ☐ Satur ☐ Sun ☐

One Goal For Today: _____

_____

_____

Today's Postive Affirmations: _____

_____

_____

_____

_____

My Mood Today: ★ ★ ★ ★ ★ ★ ★ ★ ★ ★

My Thoughts For Today: _____

_____

_____

_____

_____

What Am I Grateful For Today: _____

_____

_____

_____

What I Am Proud Of Today: _____

_____

_____

_____

My Plans For Tomorrow: _____

_____

_____

_____

Date: _____

Mon ☐ Tues ☐ Wednes ☐ Thurs ☐ Fri ☐ Satur ☐ Sun ☐

One Goal For Today: _____

_____

_____

Today's Postive Affirmations: _____

_____

_____

_____

_____

My Mood Today: ☆ ☆ ☆ ☆ ☆ ☆ ☆ ☆

My Thoughts For Today: _____

_____

_____

_____

_____

What Am I Grateful For Today: _____

_____

_____

_____

What I Am Proud Of Today: _____

_____

_____

_____

My Plans For Tomorrow: _____

_____

_____

_____

Date: _____

Mon ☐ Tues ☐ Wednes ☐ Thurs ☐ Fri ☐ Satur ☐ Sun ☐

One Goal For Today: _____

_____

_____

Today's Postive Affirmations: _____

_____

_____

_____

_____

My Mood Today: ⭐ ⭐ ⭐ ⭐ ⭐ ⭐ ⭐ ⭐ ⭐ ⭐

My Thoughts For Today: _____

_____

_____

_____

_____

What Am I Grateful For Today: _____

_____

_____

_____

What I Am Proud Of Today: _____

_____

_____

_____

My Plans For Tomorrow: _____

_____

_____

_____

Date: _____

Mon ☐ Tues ☐ Wednes ☐ Thurs ☐ Fri ☐ Satur ☐ Sun ☐

One Goal For Today: _____

_____

_____

Today's Postive Affirmations: _____

_____

_____

_____

_____

My Mood Today: ☆ ☆ ☆ ☆ ☆ ☆ ☆ ☆ ☆ ☆

My Thoughts For Today: _____

_____

_____

_____

_____

What Am I Grateful For Today: _____

_____

_____

_____

What I Am Proud Of Today: _____

_____

_____

_____

My Plans For Tomorrow: _____

_____

_____

_____

Date: _____

Mon ☐ Tues ☐ Wednes ☐ Thurs ☐ Fri ☐ Satur ☐ Sun ☐

One Goal For Today: _____

_____

_____

Today's Postive Affirmations: _____

_____

_____

_____

_____

My Mood Today: ⭐ ⭐ ⭐ ⭐ ⭐ ⭐ ⭐ ⭐ ⭐ ⭐

My Thoughts For Today: _____

_____

_____

_____

_____

What Am I Grateful For Today: _____

_____

_____

_____

What I Am Proud Of Today: _____

_____

_____

_____

My Plans For Tomorrow: _____

_____

_____

_____

Date: _____

Mon ☐ Tues ☐ Wednes ☐ Thurs ☐ Fri ☐ Satur ☐ Sun ☐

One Goal For Today: _____

_____

_____

Today's Postive Affirmations: _____

_____

_____

_____

_____

My Mood Today: ☆ ☆ ☆ ☆ ☆ ☆ ☆ ☆ ☆ ☆

My Thoughts For Today: _____

_____

_____

_____

_____

What Am I Grateful For Today: _____

_____

_____

_____

What I Am Proud Of Today: _____

_____

_____

_____

My Plans For Tomorrow: _____

_____

_____

_____

Date: _____

Mon ☐ Tues ☐ Wednes ☐ Thurs ☐ Fri ☐ Satur ☐ Sun ☐

One Goal For Today: _____

_____

_____

Today's Postive Affirmations: _____

_____

_____

_____

_____

My Mood Today: ⭐ ⭐ ⭐ ⭐ ⭐ ⭐ ⭐ ⭐ ⭐ ⭐

My Thoughts For Today: _____

_____

_____

_____

_____

What Am I Grateful For Today: _____

_____

_____

_____

What I Am Proud Of Today: _____

_____

_____

_____

My Plans For Tomorrow: _____

_____

_____

_____

Date: _____

Mon ☐ Tues ☐ Wednes ☐ Thurs ☐ Fri ☐ Satur ☐ Sun ☐

One Goal For Today: _____

_____

_____

Today's Postive Affirmations: _____

_____

_____

_____

_____

My Mood Today: ☆ ☆ ☆ ☆ ☆ ☆ ☆ ☆ ☆ ☆

My Thoughts For Today: _____

_____

_____

_____

_____

What Am I Grateful For Today: _____

_____

_____

_____

What I Am Proud Of Today: _____

_____

_____

_____

My Plans For Tomorrow: _____

_____

_____

_____

Date: _____

Mon ☐ Tues ☐ Wednes ☐ Thurs ☐ Fri ☐ Satur ☐ Sun ☐

One Goal For Today: _____

_____

_____

Today's Postive Affirmations: _____

_____

_____

_____

_____

My Mood Today: ★ ★ ★ ★ ★ ★ ★ ★ ★ ★

My Thoughts For Today: _____

_____

_____

_____

_____

What Am I Grateful For Today: _____

_____

_____

_____

What I Am Proud Of Today: _____

_____

_____

_____

My Plans For Tomorrow: _____

_____

_____

_____

Date: _____

Mon ☐ Tues ☐ Wednes ☐ Thurs ☐ Fri ☐ Satur ☐ Sun ☐

One Goal For Today: _____

_____

_____

Today's Postive Affirmations: _____

_____

_____

_____

_____

My Mood Today: ☆ ☆ ☆ ☆ ☆ ☆ ☆ ☆ ☆ ☆

My Thoughts For Today: _____

_____

_____

_____

_____

What Am I Grateful For Today: _____

_____

_____

_____

What I Am Proud Of Today: _____

_____

_____

_____

My Plans For Tomorrow: _____

_____

_____

_____

Date: _____

Mon ☐ Tues ☐ Wednes ☐ Thurs ☐ Fri ☐ Satur ☐ Sun ☐

One Goal For Today: _____

_____

_____

Today's Postive Affirmations: _____

_____

_____

_____

_____

My Mood Today: ☆ ☆ ☆ ☆ ☆ ☆ ☆ ☆ ☆ ☆

My Thoughts For Today: _____

_____

_____

_____

_____

What Am I Grateful For Today: _____

_____

_____

_____

What I Am Proud Of Today: _____

_____

_____

_____

My Plans For Tomorrow: _____

_____

_____

_____

Date: _____

Mon ☐ Tues ☐ Wednes ☐ Thurs ☐ Fri ☐ Satur ☐ Sun ☐

One Goal For Today: _____

_____

_____

Today's Postive Affirmations: _____

_____

_____

_____

_____

My Mood Today: ⭐ ⭐ ⭐ ⭐ ⭐ ⭐ ⭐ ⭐ ⭐

My Thoughts For Today: _____

_____

_____

_____

_____

What Am I Grateful For Today: _____

_____

_____

_____

What I Am Proud Of Today: _____

_____

_____

_____

My Plans For Tomorrow: _____

_____

_____

_____

Date: _____

Mon ☐ Tues ☐ Wednes ☐ Thurs ☐ Fri ☐ Satur ☐ Sun ☐

One Goal For Today: _____

_____

_____

Today's Postive Affirmations: _____

_____

_____

_____

_____

My Mood Today: ★ ★ ★ ★ ★ ★ ★ ★ ★ ★

My Thoughts For Today: _____

_____

_____

_____

_____

What Am I Grateful For Today: _____

_____

_____

_____

What I Am Proud Of Today: _____

_____

_____

_____

My Plans For Tomorrow: _____

_____

_____

_____

Date: _____

Mon ☐ Tues ☐ Wednes ☐ Thurs ☐ Fri ☐ Satur ☐ Sun ☐

One Goal For Today: _____

_____

_____

Today's Postive Affirmations: _____

_____

_____

_____

_____

My Mood Today: ☆ ☆ ☆ ☆ ☆ ☆ ☆ ☆ ☆ ☆

My Thoughts For Today: _____

_____

_____

_____

_____

What Am I Grateful For Today: _____

_____

_____

_____

What I Am Proud Of Today: _____

_____

_____

_____

My Plans For Tomorrow: _____

_____

_____

_____

Date: _____

Mon ☐ Tues ☐ Wednes ☐ Thurs ☐ Fri ☐ Satur ☐ Sun ☐

One Goal For Today: _____

_____

_____

Today's Postive Affirmations: _____

_____

_____

_____

_____

My Mood Today: ☆ ☆ ☆ ☆ ☆ ☆ ☆ ☆ ☆ ☆

My Thoughts For Today: _____

_____

_____

_____

_____

What Am I Grateful For Today: _____

_____

_____

_____

What I Am Proud Of Today: _____

_____

_____

_____

My Plans For Tomorrow: _____

_____

_____

_____

Date: _____

Mon ☐ Tues ☐ Wednes ☐ Thurs ☐ Fri ☐ Satur ☐ Sun ☐

One Goal For Today: _____
_____
_____

Today's Postive Affirmations: _____
_____
_____
_____
_____

My Mood Today: ☆ ☆ ☆ ☆ ☆ ☆ ☆ ☆ ☆ ☆

My Thoughts For Today: _____
_____
_____
_____
_____

What Am I Grateful For Today: _____
_____
_____
_____

What I Am Proud Of Today: _____
_____
_____
_____

My Plans For Tomorrow: _____
_____
_____
_____

Date: _____

Mon ☐ Tues ☐ Wednes ☐ Thurs ☐ Fri ☐ Satur ☐ Sun ☐

One Goal For Today: _____
_____
_____

Today's Postive Affirmations: _____
_____
_____
_____
_____

My Mood Today: ★ ★ ★ ★ ★ ★ ★ ★ ★ ★

My Thoughts For Today: _____
_____
_____
_____
_____

What Am I Grateful For Today: _____
_____
_____
_____

What I Am Proud Of Today: _____
_____
_____
_____

My Plans For Tomorrow: _____
_____
_____
_____

Date: _____

Mon ☐ Tues ☐ Wednes ☐ Thurs ☐ Fri ☐ Satur ☐ Sun ☐

One Goal For Today: _____

_____

_____

Today's Postive Affirmations: _____

_____

_____

_____

_____

My Mood Today: ☆ ☆ ☆ ☆ ☆ ☆ ☆ ☆ ☆ ☆

My Thoughts For Today: _____

_____

_____

_____

_____

What Am I Grateful For Today: _____

_____

_____

_____

What I Am Proud Of Today: _____

_____

_____

_____

My Plans For Tomorrow: _____

_____

_____

_____

Date: _____
Mon ☐ Tues ☐ Wednes ☐ Thurs ☐ Fri ☐ Satur ☐ Sun ☐

One Goal For Today: _____
_____
_____

Today's Postive Affirmations: _____
_____
_____
_____

My Mood Today: ★ ★ ★ ★ ★ ★ ★ ★ ★ ★

My Thoughts For Today: _____
_____
_____
_____
_____

What Am I Grateful For Today: _____
_____
_____
_____

What I Am Proud Of Today: _____
_____
_____
_____

My Plans For Tomorrow: _____
_____
_____
_____

Date: _____

Mon ☐ Tues ☐ Wednes ☐ Thurs ☐ Fri ☐ Satur ☐ Sun ☐

One Goal For Today: _____
_____
_____

Today's Postive Affirmations: _____
_____
_____
_____
_____

My Mood Today: ★ ★ ★ ★ ★ ★ ★ ★

My Thoughts For Today: _____
_____
_____
_____
_____

What Am I Grateful For Today: _____
_____
_____
_____

What I Am Proud Of Today: _____
_____
_____
_____

My Plans For Tomorrow: _____
_____
_____
_____

Date: _____

Mon ☐ Tues ☐ Wednes ☐ Thurs ☐ Fri ☐ Satur ☐ Sun ☐

One Goal For Today: _____
_____
_____

Today's Postive Affirmations: _____
_____
_____
_____
_____

My Mood Today: ⭐ ⭐ ⭐ ⭐ ⭐ ⭐ ⭐ ⭐ ⭐

My Thoughts For Today: _____
_____
_____
_____
_____

What Am I Grateful For Today: _____
_____
_____
_____

What I Am Proud Of Today: _____
_____
_____
_____

My Plans For Tomorrow: _____
_____
_____
_____

Date: _____

Mon ☐ Tues ☐ Wednes ☐ Thurs ☐ Fri ☐ Satur ☐ Sun ☐

One Goal For Today: _____
_____
_____

Today's Postive Affirmations: _____
_____
_____
_____
_____

My Mood Today: ⭐ ⭐ ⭐ ⭐ ⭐ ⭐ ⭐ ⭐ ⭐ ⭐

My Thoughts For Today: _____
_____
_____
_____
_____

What Am I Grateful For Today: _____
_____
_____
_____

What I Am Proud Of Today: _____
_____
_____
_____

My Plans For Tomorrow: _____
_____
_____
_____

Date: _____

Mon ☐ Tues ☐ Wednes ☐ Thurs ☐ Fri ☐ Satur ☐ Sun ☐

One Goal For Today: _____

_____

_____

Today's Postive Affirmations: _____

_____

_____

_____

_____

My Mood Today: ★ ★ ★ ★ ★ ★ ★ ★ ★ ★

My Thoughts For Today: _____

_____

_____

_____

_____

What Am I Grateful For Today: _____

_____

_____

_____

What I Am Proud Of Today: _____

_____

_____

_____

My Plans For Tomorrow: _____

_____

_____

_____

Date: _____

Mon ☐ Tues ☐ Wednes ☐ Thurs ☐ Fri ☐ Satur ☐ Sun ☐

One Goal For Today: _____
_____
_____

Today's Postive Affirmations: _____
_____
_____
_____
_____

My Mood Today: ☆ ☆ ☆ ☆ ☆ ☆ ☆ ☆ ☆ ☆

My Thoughts For Today: _____
_____
_____
_____
_____

What Am I Grateful For Today: _____
_____
_____
_____

What I Am Proud Of Today: _____
_____
_____
_____

My Plans For Tomorrow: _____
_____
_____
_____

Date: _____

Mon ☐ Tues ☐ Wednes ☐ Thurs ☐ Fri ☐ Satur ☐ Sun ☐

One Goal For Today: _____

_____

_____

Today's Postive Affirmations: _____

_____

_____

_____

My Mood Today: ⭐ ⭐ ⭐ ⭐ ⭐ ⭐ ⭐ ⭐ ⭐ ⭐

My Thoughts For Today: _____

_____

_____

_____

_____

What Am I Grateful For Today: _____

_____

_____

_____

What I Am Proud Of Today: _____

_____

_____

_____

My Plans For Tomorrow: _____

_____

_____

_____

Date: _____

Mon ☐ Tues ☐ Wednes ☐ Thurs ☐ Fri ☐ Satur ☐ Sun ☐

One Goal For Today: _____

_____

_____

Today's Postive Affirmations: _____

_____

_____

_____

_____

My Mood Today: ☆ ☆ ☆ ☆ ☆ ☆ ☆ ☆ ☆ ☆

My Thoughts For Today: _____

_____

_____

_____

_____

What Am I Grateful For Today: _____

_____

_____

_____

What I Am Proud Of Today: _____

_____

_____

_____

My Plans For Tomorrow: _____

_____

_____

_____

Date: _____

Mon ☐ Tues ☐ Wednes ☐ Thurs ☐ Fri ☐ Satur ☐ Sun ☐

One Goal For Today: _____

_____

_____

Today's Postive Affirmations: _____

_____

_____

_____

_____

My Mood Today: ★ ★ ★ ★ ★ ★ ★ ★ ★ ★

My Thoughts For Today: _____

_____

_____

_____

_____

What Am I Grateful For Today: _____

_____

_____

_____

What I Am Proud Of Today: _____

_____

_____

_____

My Plans For Tomorrow: _____

_____

_____

_____

Date: _____

Mon ☐ Tues ☐ Wednes ☐ Thurs ☐ Fri ☐ Satur ☐ Sun ☐

One Goal For Today: _____

_____

_____

Today's Postive Affirmations: _____

_____

_____

_____

My Mood Today: ☆ ☆ ☆ ☆ ☆ ☆ ☆ ☆ ☆

My Thoughts For Today: _____

_____

_____

_____

_____

What Am I Grateful For Today: _____

_____

_____

_____

What I Am Proud Of Today: _____

_____

_____

_____

My Plans For Tomorrow: _____

_____

_____

_____

Date: _____

Mon ☐ Tues ☐ Wednes ☐ Thurs ☐ Fri ☐ Satur ☐ Sun ☐

One Goal For Today: _____

_____

_____

Today's Postive Affirmations: _____

_____

_____

_____

_____

My Mood Today: ☆ ☆ ☆ ☆ ☆ ☆ ☆ ☆ ☆ ☆

My Thoughts For Today: _____

_____

_____

_____

_____

What Am I Grateful For Today: _____

_____

_____

_____

What I Am Proud Of Today: _____

_____

_____

_____

My Plans For Tomorrow: _____

_____

_____

_____

Date: _____

Mon ☐ Tues ☐ Wednes ☐ Thurs ☐ Fri ☐ Satur ☐ Sun ☐

One Goal For Today: _____

_____

_____

Today's Postive Affirmations: _____

_____

_____

_____

_____

My Mood Today: ☆ ☆ ☆ ☆ ☆ ☆ ☆ ☆ ☆

My Thoughts For Today: _____

_____

_____

_____

_____

What Am I Grateful For Today: _____

_____

_____

_____

What I Am Proud Of Today: _____

_____

_____

_____

My Plans For Tomorrow: _____

_____

_____

_____

Date: _____

Mon ☐ Tues ☐ Wednes ☐ Thurs ☐ Fri ☐ Satur ☐ Sun ☐

One Goal For Today: _____

_____

_____

Today's Postive Affirmations: _____

_____

_____

_____

_____

My Mood Today: ★ ★ ★ ★ ★ ★ ★ ★ ★ ★

My Thoughts For Today: _____

_____

_____

_____

_____

What Am I Grateful For Today: _____

_____

_____

_____

What I Am Proud Of Today: _____

_____

_____

_____

My Plans For Tomorrow: _____

_____

_____

_____

Date: _____

Mon ☐ Tues ☐ Wednes ☐ Thurs ☐ Fri ☐ Satur ☐ Sun ☐

One Goal For Today: _____

_____

_____

Today's Postive Affirmations: _____

_____

_____

_____

_____

My Mood Today: ⭐ ⭐ ⭐ ⭐ ⭐ ⭐ ⭐ ⭐

My Thoughts For Today: _____

_____

_____

_____

_____

What Am I Grateful For Today: _____

_____

_____

_____

What I Am Proud Of Today: _____

_____

_____

_____

My Plans For Tomorrow: _____

_____

_____

_____

Date: _____

Mon ☐ Tues ☐ Wednes ☐ Thurs ☐ Fri ☐ Satur ☐ Sun ☐

One Goal For Today: _____

_____

_____

Today's Postive Affirmations: _____

_____

_____

_____

_____

My Mood Today: ★ ★ ★ ★ ★ ★ ★ ★ ★ ★

My Thoughts For Today: _____

_____

_____

_____

_____

What Am I Grateful For Today: _____

_____

_____

_____

What I Am Proud Of Today: _____

_____

_____

_____

My Plans For Tomorrow: _____

_____

_____

_____

Date: _____

Mon ☐ Tues ☐ Wednes ☐ Thurs ☐ Fri ☐ Satur ☐ Sun ☐

One Goal For Today: _____

_____

_____

Today's Postive Affirmations: _____

_____

_____

_____

My Mood Today: ⭐ ⭐ ⭐ ⭐ ⭐ ⭐ ⭐ ⭐ ⭐

My Thoughts For Today: _____

_____

_____

_____

_____

What Am I Grateful For Today: _____

_____

_____

_____

What I Am Proud Of Today: _____

_____

_____

_____

My Plans For Tomorrow: _____

_____

_____

_____

Date: _____

Mon ☐ Tues ☐ Wednes ☐ Thurs ☐ Fri ☐ Satur ☐ Sun ☐

One Goal For Today: _____

_____

_____

Today's Postive Affirmations: _____

_____

_____

_____

_____

My Mood Today: ⭐ ⭐ ⭐ ⭐ ⭐ ⭐ ⭐ ⭐ ⭐ ⭐

My Thoughts For Today: _____

_____

_____

_____

_____

What Am I Grateful For Today: _____

_____

_____

_____

What I Am Proud Of Today: _____

_____

_____

_____

My Plans For Tomorrow: _____

_____

_____

_____

Made in the USA
Monee, IL
28 June 2022